Versions of May

Versions of May

Poems by
Jim Murphy

Negative Capability Press

Copyright 2023 Jim Murphy

First Edition

All rights reserved.

Cover Art: Melissa Murphy

Book & Cover Design: Anne Kent Rush

ISBN: 978-0-942544-17-6 Hardback
ISBN 978-0-942544-09-1 Paperback
ISBN 978-0-942544-43-5 ebook

This book is for Melissa, Norah, Wayland, Elodie and Blythe, each one and all together.

In honor of Barbara Murphy, who taught me what it truly means to stay forever young

Contents

1

Grave as Blackberries	3
El Zócalo	5
Lines on Fraktur	9
Air Travel in the Year of Our Lord	12
Letter to Westerberg	13
Sound Check with Artifacts	15
Terra Nova	16
Southern Holi	17
Too Much with Us	19

2

Foster	27
Lucky Thirteen	28
Case	29
Court Dress	30
Phone Call to Morrison	31
Subject with Höfner Bass	32
U2 Bootleg, 1989	33
Old Man with Ax Handle	34
Memento Vitae	35
The Buddha's Artillery	36
Interior with Grasshopper	37

Education with Emperor Moths	38
Creek Heart	39
Sapphire Saturday	40
When She's Ten Feet Tall	41
What Last Century Did Away with	42
Old Hundredth	43
Fled is that Music	44

3

Black Dog Crossing	47
In Defense of Chet Baker	49
Ruins Near Duy Phú	50
A Different Tack	54
Supermarine Spitfire	56
Nobody's Fault but Mine (Trad.)	58
Time's Curls and Purposes	60
Westerly	62
Author	69

1

Grave as Blackberries

Nothing like it in the world—
the way joy jumps forward

among those with little time.
Those with houses half empty,

no heirlooms, their photos
dissolved in barrels of clouds,

diplomas put to ash, theories
risen as pure smoke. It's all

free—all bonds broken, but
those of ground and sky, grave

and light, sweet and buoyant,
the way a loved one surfaces

from a dark pool, smooths back
her wet blonde hair, smiles,

rolls, then dives into the black.
That opal seam has closed,

has opened, has closed, all in
soft seconds, as when a muted

trumpet bell bows out for bass,
saxophone, and ride cymbal, then

goes forever silent. *It's not the notes
you play; it's the notes you don't

play*—Miles Davis, pharaonic,
aglow, listener in the soul's quiet

rooms, cold whirr of the air, hiss
of the tape, cloud of the stubbed

cigarette, still glass of water.
Whispers. Snaps. Taps. Begins.

El Zócalo

We walked from a sunlit
catholic hotel into the plaza,
while the twist and sway
of purposeful people moved
everywhere around us.

The National Palace was
ringed with barricades,
far across in time from us,
no way to get inside.
The crowd parted left
and right around it.

At times the enormity
of the national flag hung
limp, just a great grimace
at its downmost corners,
a gesture of forbiddance.

Among the police, candy
hawkers and the standard
street performers were
men and women arrayed

in feathers of the *Mexica,*
plumes two feet high,
they stood in structured,
atavistic masks and bracers
brocaded in black and gold.

Who were these people,
now reading the future,
now offering recitations
of the deep and shattered
past? Human thousands
walked and idled where
lakes used to feed another
capital, before the Catholic
cathedral took shape on
what was by then drained
bottomland. They placed
the red pyramidal stones
into the new framework
of their church, and then
thousands streamed inside.

There was a metal barrier.
There was a fence, a low
wall and a broad blanket
of sweet incense that drifted
visible into the raucous air.

We walked into this scene
as tourists do, and paid
a tired man to purify us.
He jumped into position
and circled you in chalk,
in words, in rapid divinity
so far beyond our lives.

He took your hands and
looked into your eyes.
We both made the nervous
laugh of the unknowing,
entertained, attempting to
participate and pay respect,
but most afraid of looking
foolish in the end. Steps
and gazes, gestures, breaths,
he worked his well-known
spell and sucked the devil
from your soul. He stooped
and chalked a powdered
circle at your feet and you
were set within a blessing
we could not even hope
to understand. There were
smiles. The sky was bright.

He lit the circle and then
flames shot up around
your body. For an instant
it seemed as if you would
dissolve as just more smoke
into the heavy summer sky.

Then with a single turn
he chanted, brushed
and killed the flames.
Something frozen began
to move again in flashes
as he cradled your fingertips
and pulled the last vestige
of infection from them.
And then the soft applause.

The scene repeated all
around, as the curious
and the faithful vied for
space. There was nothing
we could do but move
while the traffic pushed us
there to here, then to now,
forward into other histories,
no sights, no path, no guide.

Lines on Fraktur

1

This monk's discipline is to copy
some heaving sacred text by firelight.

He makes the same swift cuts with
the hollow barrel of a goose quill—

up, over, down, up—hundreds
of these angled scratches that add up

to a page, thousands, then a book,
millions more, his lifetime. In dark

lakes of ink, gray caravans of vellum,
the commitment of these ideas in

blackletter, backward-looking, slowly
cobbled from the past. Here is a key.

Here is a faun. Here is a philosophic
beard that juts from such a noble chin.

God's law conforms. These letters are
the alphabet of protest. How the people

take them is beyond his ken. He only
copies. He only circulates the current.

2

This politician's largesse is to foster
dreams of greatness under torchlight.

He oils the barrels of machine pistols
and encourages the goose steps across

plazas—left, right, left, right—scores
of troopers that add up to a platoon,

hundreds, then, a company, thousands
more, his dark regime. In hot broadcasts

over radio, hard modern angles caught
on film, the expression of these ideas

in black armbands, sideways-looking,
constructed out of loss and paranoia.

Here is a woman. Here is a Socialist.
Here is a clean-shaven face that could be

anyone's at all. Man's law breaks down.
These letters are the alphabet of chaos.

How the people scramble them is
supremely in his ken. He wills them

forward. He instigates a future where
no one can trace just how this came about.

Air Travel in the Year of Our Lord

Curve of the sunset, sweep of the runway,
sip of the river, dominion over the earth—
delete our presence here, and free us from
    ourselves.

This is how every primal break
from land and daylight comes with loss,
how crude oil still lights our children's reading
lessons, how the distances between us must
    be closed at catastrophic price.

And even so,
they open once again. The script contains
all the needed fissures and the cracks in sense.

The flight to Heathrow's overbooked. Anticipation
turned to trash, we trudge across the tiles
    to yet another car.
Something is broken here.

Back home, we wake in the dark, trying to be sure—
There's the rustle and crunch of leaves in wind,
the oily petrichor, then the flare of gentle rain.

Letter to Westerberg

When I started this, I tried to be myself,
tried not to think about the maze of states

between us, the forever X'ed out calendar
of achievement long left on the dirty floor

while the children grew, while the new life
took root and began to thrive. And yet here

I am, back in the damaged and distorted
record that you left like blood on snow,

like belief in a sinking ship, like the last
day of 1959. When I got to the middle part,

I thought about a ringing night at Mabel's
in Champaign when you could have been

Jack Kerouac in bowling shoes. All that
time I thought no one in the room but us

knew a single damn thing about anyone
else's suffering. That's an untrue thing.

So sometimes I hate what I have made,
when I've tried to sing something so past

art that the attempt shot low and left
everything else so merely literary it was

a fucking embarrassment. But still, here
at the end of this, a nod and handshake

for the spirit to smolder, to mumble praise
despite the fires behind you. I don't know

just who you are, or who I am, if I am true,
except over the haunted air. Sincerely.

Sound Check with Artifacts

I must remember reappearance
is not reunion, to reawaken not
a Holy Resurrection. Here, in fits

and starts, the faded curtains part
to life. The footlights sear the dark
dust and air, a theater of tone comes

open. Here we are once more, this
unsteady gift and us—so many years
to earn a decent, undramatic name—

like *Lou Reed* —so earthbound and so
mixed with pretense. I mean the man,
not the character in shades, exactly,

who wandered through identities
with a simple New York shrug.
We make up the real and crackle

the static, and *on that New York station,
she just didn't believe what she heard at all.*
That fine, fine music. Is that enough?

Terra Nova

One moment after the telescope,
after months of panicked prayer
below decks and much first-rate
speech above, the dark imagined
end of things—ghost ship lost
to myth or history—has vanished.

In an instant, she's spared for some
other fate, as through the blue-green
mist the captain's hard left eye
now blinks and squints, and the lies
passed on for generations tumble
dead down to the waves. No mistake

as the coast opens up before him.
The land—a burst of narrow beach,
a fusillade of gray jungle, and a dark
mountain chain that leaps up from
the sand—nothing known for sure
except the sweet terror of horizons.

Southern Holi

When the color dust exploded overhead
in puffs of electric blue, red, green and gold,
our four children spun with sudden laughter,
in a haze of pure happiness because they had
stumbled into something utterly unknown
and found joy there. The air was complicated
by some questions. The noon light was filtered
with filaments of the distant past and we were
ignorant of it, lost in the compact present.

On the other side of what we did not see,
we ran our hands through currents and made
streams where the color followed dipping hands.
We walked through doors of ridiculousness
and bliss, hopped on one foot across tradition.
For you and me there was a hitch. There was
an embarrassed instant of the Raj, a hint of
Mountbatten in his coat of dismal medals.
There were unheard calls from unknown voices
in the atmosphere, and so right then we halted.

But the children spun, and ran, and roared
across the cordoned lot along with scores

of others. Nothing froze in them. No worries
about propriety or place. They just ducked
into the crowd and vanished in the safety
there. We found one with feet in the fountain,
one at the edge of traffic, one sitting on a chain,
the last one looking for ice cream. It was a day
for good, not evil, not a worry in the world.

Too Much with Us

> *"We have given our hearts away"*
> *- William Wordsworth*

1

We had infallible August afternoons, when
Columbia, Missouri grew to worldly size.
Our sodden, east side block of it was studded
with all these moldy houses that had been
left to someone's eldest child, then some years
later rented out to piss-poor undergrads.

I later wondered what our landlord,
respectable daughter of the flat Midwest,
thought when she would intermittently inspect
her fleabag house, find bugs and bottles,
so many inchoate stains on the walls of rooms
where she learned to read, slept in innocence,
was taught manners, and learned to play piano.
It might have been a slow bomb dropped
through her memories. It might have been
disgust with the piglets who rooted in her home.
It might have been we were walking dollar signs.
Two years and she never had the shower fixed.

When we finally went back there after forty,
the windows' film of soot was just the same.

2

I improved my focus somewhat in Ohio.
This was a time I was told there were journals
far back in the stacks of the modern disaster
that was the library with pages razored out,
carrels with all the books spine-in, so no other
grad student would ever find them. Was it true?
What did it matter when the sudden, ugly
gleam of envy shone in all our darting eyes?
We were well-trained into a state of nature
where fear and *Schadenfreude* made us titter
in high civility when someone failed their test,
or someone went home with the professor
of political science, who chain smoked
all morning in her office, with twisting shapes
that slowly rose, then vanished into nothing.
He said the coffee that they had next morning
was the most bitter thing he'd ever tasted.
Because of these lessons, I had to run
three miles a day, bike two, and drink enough
at night to slam bewilderment to the back
of my mind, to the back of the pool hall, where
I played one black song after another, thinking

someone, someday would hear. But I ran out
of quarters every time and then wobbled
into the quiet night of dark bungalows where
working people slept, fed up and exhausted.
At that time, the only drivers who hissed up
Hamilton Ave. were cops or those who feared them.
We became willing clients of order and of money
while we were dressed in thrift store clothes.

3

We drove down to take the temperature
of our miracle small town. I had won
a kind of lottery. I wore that fact on my face
like a simple man's grin and thought it was
good humor. We were introduced to weathers
and to foods with long and stormy histories,
to unspoken codes we hadn't ever truly heard
in the poems or the songs. I bought a new
leather bag and stuffed it with ambition.
I wore good clothes and showed up early.
The halls reeked of cleaning fluid and must
have been the sparkling dream of someone
who was in charge of the academic buildings,
the college grounds so impeccable and green.
The Realtor met us at the hazy corner
where Main Street met Nabors, and then

invited us into her enormous Lincoln SUV.
We rode slowly through the place, and on
almost every block she gently pointed out
the house of some old friend. The beauty
in this should not be underrated. She *belonged*.
We wanted to be happy then and thought
that we would be. Up and down all afternoon,
ten miles per hour. Her winding stories never
stopped. But most of what we saw was out
of range. In the bank's pine-paneled offices,
there was a signature line that would deduct us,
so we were trying to be sure. We noticed a house
in the glossy booklet that was left out of our tour,
one with a bright description that ticked off all
our wishes and was so *reasonable*, we thought
we had a secret. At the time we weren't too
subtle, so I insisted that we go. The Realtor
picked up speed. She drove us far out, past
the golf course, past impossible horse farms
with their perfect paths and fences, over a rise,
until we reached kudzu. And then she offered us
her token: *I just want you to see what's out here.
I just want you to look around.* And so we did.
And the horizon quickly tightened to a point,
to a hilltop where that little house was waving,
while beaten shacks sat scattered all around
in a listless maze of hard times, chronic, broken

trailers and a rusty clutch of dead machines.
So smart, I couldn't think of anything to say.

4

Years later, in the city, cocooned in tenure,
always more lucky than I was wise, I clicked
on the last bastion, *The New York Times*,
pulled sweet fresh fruit from our battleship
refrigerator, and let the early quiet gather
family around me, to my heart before my eyes.
A true woman I loved was asleep in our bed,
four dear children still dreaming each in theirs.
The spark and rumble of the A/C kicking on
was a muted mantra. It was here. It was now.
And outside, in the wild, bursting garden,
bathed in sunlight, a massive king snake slithered.
The New York Times rarely runs a story on
the king snake, friend to humankind, deliverer
from poisons large and small. The huge snake
did not need me to kill it, so I stayed captive
in the house and watched it go its silent way.
Back with the *Times*, I read a long feature
on the housing situation, well-researched,
with reporting from three states. It concerned
constriction of the market, and the lack
of opportunities therein. How new tactics

now were needed. How a lucky few had found
forever homes despite these trends. One chipper
couple had rented a hovel in a college town
and waited for the owner to die. They made
her cookies and brought iced tea, offered
to mow the rangy lawn and replace the dripping
fixtures. They hired men to do these things
and checked Zillow every day. In another place,
a couple didn't mind that an accidental fire
had happened in their hallway. *We got it
for a song. A roomy third floor walk-up in a boho
part of town. So cute and near to everything.*
They performed a smudge and moved right in.
Even a preacher of no known denomination,
transferred from California to the South, found
what the Lord had willed: A proud hill out
in the country. He would build a mansion there,
where once was only sin. The land was cheap,
he had loans from three finance companies
and there were complex mechanisms. He had
his family in tow and his congregation was elated.
*Getting and spending, we lay waste our powers--
Little we see in Nature that is ours.*

2

Foster

Begin again with breath, always a small
star of being within you. Begin with
the heart, the sound, the sight of early
sun or late rain, the wheels of summer
that tumble forward into fall. Begin in
the crystalline present, the chrysalis
of the next moment, and the soft beds
where our children sleep well-tended
by the future, by their future. We foster
hope each time we walk the stones
before us. Blue music ushers us into
a country still unseen. But we have
been here. We've felt it with our hands.

Lucky Thirteen

It's no good. I cannot shake and roll
you—the best I do is come up twelve.
You clatter in my fist like small frozen
ghosts—lovely friends and former selves
reduced to chance, then elevated to this
nothingness. When I believed that I
could win, I bet it all. When I believed
that I had lost, I won it back twice over.
You were bones, then snowfall, teeth,
then melting ice. You were the hot luck
that no one ever has for long, and then
you got much warmer. The roll alone
is why you're here, never high enough.

Case

It's in there. At last, I know it truly is—
a thing lit from inside, as if flame
itself had hardened into brass, or gold
had captured the plastic nature of rain.
But why does it vanish when the lid
is lifted? All these overseas stamps
said the case had come so far. These
dents and scratches told me things
I recognized on greed and violence.
The latches were fox-traps where I
paid for legal help on the imagination
of yours and mine. It all made sense,
just like pouring light into a suitcase.

Court Dress

When I was a judge, I wore fine ermine, silk,
and a heavy wig that scrolled my shoulders.
I was correct, and the whiskey of decision
kept me warm. When I was a prosecutor,
I sported a charcoal suit and tie, and waved
legal papers high to prove that I was right.
By then the cold cocaine of victory had made
me unreachable. And when I was condemned,
after my arrest, walking among the scaffolds
and cells I made myself, I cried unneeded tears
until the sweet heroin of loss took my breath.
There was no more. Now, in silent heaven
I'm mostly sober, and I mostly just go nude.

Phone Call to Morrison

As if there was a way to talk about it.
I still want more than this joss stick that
I burned myself at age fourteen, more
than the acid I took when I fell through
the ice of your record. I demand more
because you wanted me to be exactly this,
someone looking up at chaos. But aren't
we all? You were totally lost and found
in the screaming ocean of Ray's Vox organ,
and deserted roads, empty movie houses,
so many blue hotels. There's just no way.
I'm trying to reach you on a black phone
in the hall, hung by its neck until dead.

Subject with Höfner Bass

Even now, it stands apart from him, cornered
in the same black coffin. Even if he pops the clips
and plays until he makes the grooves hum back
for the dog or fifty thousand people, the silence
before and after is the only place he finds himself.
He's ruined every coat he owns, always carrying
a pen or two for the hopeless autograph dream
crash on a bus, or in the sky, where nobody
knows exactly if it's him. He's let go the false
mustache, the dark glasses, and the other names.
Time lets him arrive here on his own. The past
is back there—the heavy spruce and maple body,
a faded short setlist, the far-off glow of vacuum tubes.

U2 Bootleg, 1989

Someone had a black cassette with nothing written on the label. We were shocked somehow that the sound was muddy blank, our heroes lost as we were in the new wine of their German songs. They transmitted from somewhere free that barely yet existed. They were with us as we tugged on belts and buttons, with jingled drops and tension pops of pure surprise. It was yearbook time when no thought or faith could help what we were going to become. Someone fired up a soul. Someone laughed. It was entirely ok—we denied the darkness and lay down.

Old Man with Ax Handle

Thirty-six stout inches of American hickory—
freighted with all-conquering fear, my neighbor,
you carry it daily at your side as you negotiate
the simple paths of quietude. What animals
retreat before you—timid herons, mild mutts
and cats—it's not these that bring you battle.
So where's the man that you will hammer?
In 1969, did he walk into a bar in melting daylight,
just like now, and never come out again? Did he
cringe at the joke you told in the dark? Nothing
doing out here today. Your projected fury is
enough to push back any comers. Where are you
going with that weapon? Where have you been?

Memento Vitae

> *On Learning a Portion of Adolf Hitler's Skull*
> *Was Recovered by Soviet Forces*

Years later, after the Party functions
where he would gesture darkly toward
the past, then bring it out of secrecy,
uncork the rumor, hold it up as proof
the system worked, after vodka toasts
and red, sweat-damp congratulations,
after he gloried in it with his mistress,
clarified for her the truth, palmed her
head, and swelled in self, after he spat
on it, slathered it in every insult, there
it remained—frozen in a globe of glass,
that human jawbone, once also capable
of words, now meaningless as mastery.

The Buddha's Artillery

It all seemed like war and chaos there—
a landscape that appeared to be just blank
ribcages and broken skulls. We heard
the drum of shells and were about to drop.
The wind went quiet and the sky became
a furious blue. And they rose, and knit up
suddenly before us—splinters into tree limbs,
tattered uniforms and bloody battle flags
unweaved back into cloudy cotton. A flock
of birds raced backward, then their pale
eggs dropped one by one down to the earth.
In the pattern of that soft, crackling rain,
we were children, and we could barely stand.

Interior with Grasshopper

The stakes are low. The scale is small.
The year is nodding slowly into fall, when
in our country all the rituals of harvest are
enacted on the web—cookies and cartoons
pop up for everyone—all who have been
spooked into belief in the unnatural. It rises
gory, like the smoke of oil and rubber from
a dead car by the highway. A thinking human
can become by itself a smoking ruin, stuck
in neutral. Then you suddenly arrive—you
green trick of light and sky, all by yourself,
you clamber down my shirt and seek your
nature there, where I'd almost forgotten it.

Education with Emperor Moths

Ten years old, and in this instant, your future
draws you like white, fast-burning paraffin.
All the firm and stern ones who pushed you
here, made for you a present of unbelievable
promise, tied your hair with strips of wishes,
and braided you into their dreams—where
are they now? No road before you, only light,
and dark behind—you're choiceless in the joy
between. And here you burst yourself in two.
Yourselves lean both left and right, almost
free from the flutter of wings, the false eyes
planted on your back. Their crowded patronage
confounds you, a column of smoke in your sky.

Creek Heart

At the center, a stone—a wave of ages since
light found shell, and sand, and natural
hunger took in all besides—pebbled in
red and green, a concretion of the possible
you frame upon your chest. Your index finger,
rose gold ringed and nimble, must have dug
into the cold, clear ambience of dreaming,
drew the heart out into your palm, and lifted it
dripping to your breastbone. Your skin still
holds the sunlight. Lips just open, birthing
a whistle, or a kiss. And for a fragile moment,
you are in the systole and diastole of rushing
water, still summer, yet ankle-deep in snow.

Sapphire Saturday

She roller-skated backward, out of the past
in neon knee pads and a tight t-shirt, singing
"I Can't Go for That"—Oh no-oh, no can do—
and blew past me like I wasn't even moving.
Her difficulties knew no end, and I listened
to her poems of foaming stallions, chariots
that jumped in olive groves, out of control
sports cars, and nosedives in shot-up planes,
abbreviated kisses, going down. This went on
some time. It was late. She didn't have to say
she didn't think so. My compass spun with
what was hidden. As she left, she said *You can
call me Sapphire, or just Sappho if you want.*

When She's Ten Feet Tall

The seizing sputter of aimless words has stopped
for now. Between us, only pulsing trill and drone—
cloudy bee, tear drop sitar, strange bloody stream.
What were we dreaming when the light came on
and the wicked horns of panic pushed us both back
into silence? You knocked your bruised forehead
into every black door frame. You shook your fist
at our altitude, then were higher than any aircraft
known to humankind. At last, there was nothing
left to feel up there in the sterile vaults of heaven.
Rabbits all over the cockpit, we giggled that sex
was better than it, and then left each other wilted.
I shrank by almost half, and you were almost giant.

What Last Century Did Away with

> *"Either it's raining or I'm dreaming."*
> *-François Truffaut's "Jules et Jim"*

We have much less time to kneel and weep
in the universal dark beside our beds. Today
that's all done in brushed nickel bathrooms,
as we hover by the sinks of dreams, defunct
along with the Third Republic, Buddy Holly,
and every dog ever fed by Pablo Picasso in
the tormented throes of genius. There, or else
in someone's sticky kitchen. *Marlon Brando,
won't you pass the marmalade?* This is what
we'd do—ask these insufferable questions of
each other while saxophones blared so loud,
we had to ask them twice. The beams were
breaking overhead. The stars were only nice.

Old Hundredth

In the disorderly decade of the 1970s,
when my father had church, he mostly
did so with cheap beer and Beethoven.
Sometimes there was Burgundy wine.
Sometimes there was Tchaikovsky, too.
But every time, the night sky itself rose
then fell with orchestrated crescendos.
And the years flew apart, side by side,
measure by measure. And his time was
kept by far off maestros, his orchestras
obscure as *Hocus Pocus* muttered under
breath. Always. What did it matter to
him—all creatures here, below praise?

Fled is That Music

For my mother, Barbara Murphy, 1937-2017

The day you left this world, we listened
to The Beatles. Slow, pure clouds curled
through the tracks, and so I let them play.
You hadn't spoken in two days. Hadn't had
a sip to drink in three. When did your eyes
close to this version of May? What poured
through? The view was an incendiary green,
too good to hide with treatments. There,
in the sunlit door you slept a hundred times.
There, in the space between, you greeted
me and saw your father. A huge sky blew
all these times together, as music of the self
relented. At last, you had become the chords.

3

Black Dog Crossing

Look. What's a two-lane road to him?
And what's a ditch? A curb? A broken line
to designate it's safe to pass? It's difficult

at best to judge without lapsing into fallacy.
And yet I do. Because I have been educated
in the judgment of everything from dactyls

to ducks to jam, the proper way to meditate,
even what to tell one's children when the dog
dies and their minds go numb with grief.

It's all like today. All like this plodding rain
and the slap-back of the windshield wipers,
metronomes for a slow, malignant tune.

Whoever is the DJ in this place should turn
the record over, pull the plug, unlove that
sleepy track and cue up something better,

something not so down. But still it comes,
and still this black dog in the bushes waits,
barely seen, but focused on the steady

rain and scalloped waves that fan the road.
I can't say what he's thinking now, or if he
knows just what to do, or if it's all the same—

the waiting and the running, the hunger
and the meal, the silence and the howling.
In the end, it's all his drive and mine,

uncomprehending, independent of each
other, but together for a flash in time
it seems, with our two ways intersecting.

Is he hungry? Out there all alone? This
is the way things start. All this driving
danger. *Good dog. Stay where you are.*

In Defense of Chet Baker

You don't need me
and you never did

need anyone to speak
up for you in the middle

of a pointless crime.
Never needed anyone

to fix your smashed teeth
or your ice cold eyes

once they came awake
and found the focal

point in middle distance
where all that dark joy

resides. Nah, you don't
need that bad business

anymore, and who am I
to remind you it's 1:30

in the universe and it's
all bright as day besides?

You just play. You just
tra-la-la with all your might.

You hear that? Someone
somewhere is singing.

Ruins Near Duy Phú

We slowly rumbled into a chain
that meant the end of the road.

Mid-morning, and condensation
curls rose through the foliage

on either side. Our guide spoke
fine English with an Australian

accent. We were in the country
that your father knew from 1969,

knew from trails like this one,
trails he walked with a briefcase

chained to one hand and a .45
steady in the other. What did

the tree line have to say when
he came and went with the other

millions of Americans? What
changed here? We walked into

the sun-lit clearing, and were told
that here the Kings of Champa

in their most blessed armor built
shrines to all that life could offer,

and honored the guises of *Shiva*,
maker of the world, destroyer of sin.

The royal stele read in cracked
Sanskrit *Out of compassion for me*

do not destroy what I have given.
And so the temples and tombs

grew outward from the center.
Waves of people seeking shelter,

centuries of peace. Eventually
the *Viet Cong* also took rest among

the stones, and must have also
marveled at the intricate reliefs

carved there. Who ran his fingers
over the words and wondered?

Who ordered the daylight mission
that came out of the dreaming

sky to obliterate the centuries'
solemnity, to reduce almost every

structure to powder? The ruins
were crumbled and overgrown.

A chain of dud bombs testified
to the victory of fear, of doubt.

What changed there? We came.
We vanished. We left in silence.

A Different Tack

Once he sailed his adult life
into a basement and a bag,
into a mine so black and deep,
the sun was in another time
zone high above him. Others
joked that high pay and long
hours left them with nothing
else to do but adulterate their
marriages in the tilt to night,
gone then from almost empty
bars to almost empty motels
and then down to dreamless
sleep. He left that talk right
where it was. He took the next
flight home to see his girls.
Things went well for a while.
Flames glowed around the bit
as the coal exhaled methane
so far beneath the surface.
From time to time, a breeze
carried ocean sweetness to
his bearded face, and happy
soothing music played on his

radio. The route moved like a barometer. Nothing stayed put for long, no matter what they told him. His truck cut through flooding in the dark. And he found his own way back to another, long lost lot.

Supermarine Spitfire

Lobed, low wings of this,
the most beautiful killing
machine ever dreamed.
This, the somehow quaint
single-seat, Rolls-Royce
flying chariot of murder—
you've lulled the hobbyists
years later into nostalgia,
into thoughts of dire wolves
just outside the sheepfold,
the cross-hatched green
and brown fields, the keen
black eyes of loyal hounds—
as if a fairy-tale had been
drawn out in the clouds over
England, and at the happy end
the good king had prevailed,
as if no rusty hand had reached
to mute your engine's rumble,
and your long declining curve
from altitude had not been
flattened utterly in time.
You've long settled down

in the gallery of just causes,
the vault of clean conscience,
a mere model, put together
by forgetful old men, alone,
who in your time were only
children, and who believed
their ears—every barked alarm,
every bullet, and every bomb.

Nobody's Fault but Mine (Trad.)

And then there was Blind Willie Johnson,
burned by the sun or burned by his stepmother,
in a moment dropped into darkness, delivered
with a Bible and a creaking cigar box guitar
on to other things—flat fees instead of royalties,
preaching in the House of Prayer, the house
fire that left him living in its ruins, deadly sick
and exposed, denied a bed, then lowered into
a lost grave. They put a plaque up in his honor.

And then there was Nina Simone, sounding
the acoustics of the hall and altering her sound
in accordance, like putting a handful of diamonds
on a scale to dim or burnish their disloyal shine.
Their weight was glossed to perfection, her voice
up in the rafters, down in the highball glasses,
everywhere possible for it to be. And the song
gathered death around it. And she pivoted again
to meet those blues with courage and in pain.

And then there was the black and white child
prodigy James Page, reborn in a satin jacket,
garlanded in the poppies that had worked into
his soul, mystified, flanged and dragging hard
on a half-burnt cigarette while his injured singer
delivered from a wheelchair. The song was done
an injury again, drug sick, spread thin as faith
in a contract with the devil. They left the church
but kept the hell. It was anonymous and long ago.

Time's Curls and Purposes

For Gunnar Pittman, 2016-2019

This is the sandy, brushed-almond dawn.
Here are rays in distant treetops, blinking

slowly awake from their dreams. Water
moves beside the boats, clear and sweet,

summer everlasting. Here are blue spruce
and white pine. Here are slips of iridescent

fish, and all the red wings blazing. Here are
strong arms and brambly beards of fathers,

the joy-lit eyes of mothers, the gentle laugh
of sisters. Here we are together. Today is

a place we have believed in, worked hard
and bartered for, almost all our lives. We

didn't know it when you found us, opened
your blue, sure eyes on this world, and all

but told us *Buckle in! We're going all the way.*
Today we know the lesson. Here and now

within the stillness, as our sense of time
falls far away, miles made of inch-stones,

every one, in all directions, here and now.
You laugh behind your wheel and drive,

windspeed in your curls, thrill of water
in your eyes. We join you in your courage.

Gunnar, bold warrior, we're all with you now.

Westerly

> "Coming down the mountain,
> one of many children..."
> -Jane's Addiction

1

Portland, Oregon, your roses buoyant
as young poems in the spring. How
time out of mind it is to brightly channel
Whitman here, addressing cities as if
they are close friends. They're more
than that—constellated attainments,
anthill dreams—*Or is it all flashes and specks?*
He wrote. *If they are not flashes and specks,
what are they?* The men and women
of Portland, Oregon, gathered in holy
cement rondure in the rain. Boom-box
and puppy-in-a-suitcase pavement
dances. Plastic drums and runaway,
half-forgotten tunes of 1999. Sunshine
where you are, listen, you, how from this
yellow rusty microbus your sandalwood
flutes whistle *tooty-toot* to starry ashes.
Inhale deep and look how loose she spins.

2

We reached Mt. St. Helens much later
in the day, with laughter and debate.
The ocean was miles off, and the Pacific
rains pummeled the hood and burst
the windshield with their thousands
of small, clear blossoms from Japan.
Communion clicks on an incline, how
we drove broadly through kaleidoscopic
fog and sun, as we together rattled off
one eastern chain and then another.
Then there were the headlit trees. We
rounded a corner and then there still
were the spent bodies of the trees, long
toppled, palmate in the cold, clear dark.
To think the earth did this. In our vision
the fallen forest slid in joy and innocence
down the mountainside of chalky umber.
There was no feeling in this. All of us were
numb. We had stopped talking long ago,
long before we got back on the highway.

3

State Park, old gold and tree trunk dusky
signage looming in the headlights. *Time
for a good soak*, he said. We all uncurled
from the car into a cool night, and with
some difficulty took the pale white trail.
Not far ahead, the sound of grown men
laughing, and the clank of bottles, plus
some distorted hippie music, vague fallout
of the Grateful Dead. Those graybeards
indefatigable in their sly, persistent glee.
We emerged into the clearing there
and saw them, pale skin lit by lanterns,
bellied by steam and wine. The tubs were
full and splashing over giddy, four men
and three women, every roundness pinked
by steam heat—soft as newborns, boundless.
I could not imagine a place more opposite
from who or what I was that night, frozen
still in my steps while my friends stripped
down and ran to them. Goddamn—the joy
and complete freedom that exploded from
them, not one over twenty-nine, as they
burst screaming from their clothes. And I
did not move a muscle. What leash snapped
tight behind me? Was it John Calvin's

heavy hand that grasped it, the red shame
or white pride of fathers? *Have you turned
into some kind of queer?* they would say, as if
some kind of instantaneous defense they
made up for themselves. *A man does not run
naked in the park with other men.* Point being,
the force of all that unknown fear, wound
tight and crystal clear, had stopped me cold.
That night as the tinkling stars splashed on,
broader minds than mine let something go
that took me another decade to understand.
It was there in the clouds of steam, there under
fragrant cedar, without effort in the night.

4

In North Beach, forty years too late, the real
estate is a privileged escarpment where poets
used to break rules, saxophones and drums,
and publish in the old way, so the cops could
take the copies and think they'd won a war.
We were always on a treasure hunt. We ran
around the country and wound up in the same
black chairs with the same black coffee, small
and strong, waiting for the pills to take, or for
the night to fall. *Allen Ginsberg Urinated Here.*
And who were we not to praise every holy

drop, not to bathe our cloudy minds in what
we should have known was only the lately
lucky karma of America. The so-happy
dribble we wrote in the Café Trieste, on
napkins, on the floor—it must have been
the fifteenth layer—we prized it, carried it
like rolls of shiny quarters in our fists.
When we find it in this century, it reads
like postcards from those former selves.
How are you, my friend? The unsure scrawl
begins. *Do you remember when we took that trip
out West? That time we saw it all? Don't laugh.
You paid for it. And I still have your address.*

Author

Jim Murphy is also the author of poetry collections *The Memphis Sun, Heaven Overland* and *The Uniform House*. He lives in Birmingham, Alabama and is Professor of English at the University of Montevallo.

Acknowledgments

Thanks to the editors of *Birmingham Poetry Review, Jabberwock Review, Poetry South* and *Steel Toe Review*, where certain of these poems previously appeared, sometimes in different form.

Thanks also to TJ Beitelman and Jeffrey Thomson for their feedback.

Special thanks to Sue Brannan Walker for her support of my work.

Praise for Jim Murphy's *Versions of May*

In Jim Murphy's masterful collection of poems, *Versions of May*, we catch the ordinary in the act of becoming archetype. This happens in language that summons Lou Reed, Wordsworth, and Miles Davis, whom Murphy quotes: "It's not the notes you play, it's the notes you don't." Here, it's both, with nothing "merely literary." I think this book should be announced on the sides of barns, like *See Natural Bridge* used to be. These poems are natural bridges between sensing and knowing, seeing and telling, understanding and judgment. They settle nothing, celebrate much.

Angela Ball, Center for Writers,
University of Southern Mississippi

Jim Murphy proclaims himself "always more lucky than wise," but he writes about his lucky life with rueful wisdom, even as his tender love for family and the simple delights of daily life are constantly intruded on by the poet's keen and pained awareness of the great machinations of the larger world and history's depredations on happiness, which despite everything remains happiness, and *Versions of May* acknowledges it as such. This book is a "script that contains all the needed fissures and the cracks in sense" joyfully and with great artistry.

> Andrew Hudgins, Author of *A Clown at Midnight* and *The Joker: A Memoir*

In *Versions of May* we are pushed from our present moments "forward into other histories, no sights, no path, no guide." Every poem is a little trip, visiting cathedrals, temples, tombs, battlefields, forests, and creeks, and with every stop, there is an opportunity to "delete our presence here, and free us from ourselves." What comes after we are gone charts the pulse of this collection. When the poet communes with his troubled heroes Lou Reed, Miles Davis, Jim Morrison, and many more, we have fleeting moments of understanding that are easy and pure, just like "pouring light into a suitcase." And in the spirit of passing it on, passing it down, passing it forward, we are given hope that the greats that came before us can hear us and that when we die, we'll all "become the chords." With both vastness and precision, Jim Murphy peers between the notes for the universal mysteries that happen when you are looking the other way.

> Elizabeth Hughey, Author of *White Bull*

www.ingramcontent.com/pod-product-compliance
Lightning Source LLC
Chambersburg PA
CBHW072104290426
44110CB00014B/1817